'E

LANGUAGE DIFFICULTIES IN EDUCATION

SPEECH & LANGUAGE DIFFICULTIES IN EDUCATION

Approaches to collaborative practice for teachers and speech & language therapists

PAM FLEMING

CAROL MILLER

JANNET WRIGHT

WINSLOW

Telford Road • Bicester
Oxon OX6 0TS • UK

First published in 1997 by
Winslow Press Ltd, Telford Road, Bicester, Oxon OX6 0TS

002-3394/Printed in the United Kingdom

British Library Cataloguing in Publication Data
Fleming, Pam
    Speech & language difficulties in education: approaches
    to collaborative practice for teachers and speech &
    language therapists
    1. Speech disorders in children 2. Language disorders in
    children 3. Handicapped children — Education
    I. Title II. Miller, Carol, 1944- III. Wright, Jannet A.
    371.9'142

ISBN 0 86388 182 3

Contents

Biographies

Pam Fleming is service co-ordinator for the Speech & Language Service in East Sussex Education Authority. She is a tutor to the professional development programme in Speech & Language Difficulties at the University of Birmingham and is also a member of the AFASIC advisory committee.

Carol Miller is a senior lecturer in the School of Education, University of Birmingham where she is involved in research and professional development activities in speech & language difficulties in education.

Jannet Wright is a senior lecturer in the Department of Human Communication Science, University College London and is responsible for the continuing education programmes. Her research interests include the ways in which teachers and speech & language therapists work together.

Introduction

A NUMBER OF DEVELOPMENTS over recent years have contributed to the thinking behind this booklet. Emphasis on integrated and inclusive education means that children with a wider range of abilities are likely to be found in all schools. Their entitlement to a broad and balanced curriculum suggests that, wherever possible, their needs will be met in a mainstream school. Children will be supported in their learning in school by professionals in addition to their teachers. Where children experience difficulties in language and communication, speech and language therapists may provide support and therefore work alongside teachers and other educational practitioners.

In 1993, the College of Speech and Language Therapists held a Policy Review Forum to address some of the issues for speech and language therapists working in education. Amongst the main conclusions of the forum was a strong desire to work co-operatively with others in education and for teachers and therapists to undertake joint professional development (College of Speech and

Language Therapists, 1993). A similar theme emerged from research in Scotland to investigate the role of speech and language therapists in education. In their report, Reid *et al* (1996) concluded that there was a need for a shared framework between education staff and therapists in working with speech and language difficulties.

Other developments, too, have influenced thinking. The publication of the *Code of Practice on the Identification and Assessment of Special Educational Needs* (Department for Education, 1994) highlights the importance of early identification of difficulties in school and ways in which schools can address them. The publication of principles for educational provision for children and young people with speech and language difficulties (AFASIC/ICAN, 1996) endorses strongly the need for joint training and practice for teachers and therapists.

Currently, approximately 70 per cent of speech and language therapists work with children (Enderby & Emerson, 1995). Although not all of these are necessarily in educational settings because many will be in health-based pre-school services, school-based therapy is clearly an important area of professional activity. We believe that there is now a climate which more positively encourages speech and language therapists to work in educational settings and to work collaboratively with others.

The aim of this booklet is to support speech and language therapists, teachers and other professionals who work together in educational settings. We also acknowlededge that parents and families are essential partners in this work, but the booklet does not set out to address this specifically. We hope that the themes of the booklet will promote understanding between practitioners and result in more effective provision for children.

Background

Until 1974, speech therapists were employed by health and education services. After that date, when the National Health Service underwent a reorganization, speech therapy services became the responsibility of the National Health Service. Thus the managers of speech therapy services had a unified service with which to provide therapy across both education and health for people of all ages who had communication problems. Today, despite changes in the organization of the health service, the majority of speech and language therapists who work with children are still employed by the NHS.

Statutory responsibility for provision for children with speech and language difficulties in the UK therefore lies with both health and educational services and the different employment of practitioners may need careful consideration when planning services for children. The *Code of Practice* (Department for Education, 1994) states that speech and language therapy may be regarded as either educational or non-educational provision, depending on the circumstances of each individual case. It states that, while it is the responsibility of health services to provide therapy, if they do not do so the ultimate responsibility lies with education authorities (*ibid*, 1994, para IV:34).

The introduction of Local Management of Schools (LMS) has resulted in greater autonomy of individual schools, where the head and governors are responsible for managing the school budget. Health service managers may therefore find themselves having to negotiate directly with schools rather than with a larger body.

Health and education services provide somewhat different contexts for practitioners, which may sometimes obstruct collaboration between them. However, the report of the Scottish study (Reid *et al*, 1996) concluded that many of the current disadvantages of working in health could be dealt with in the contracting arrangements between education authorities and speech and language therapy providers or at the level of arrangements between individual therapists and schools.

Initial professional education

Although teaching and speech and language therapy are both all-graduate professions, the nature of the initial professional education can be very different and, indeed, may be thought of as developing different 'cultures'. Each has its own language and vocabulary which may be difficult for others to understand. Professional training may have led them to think and work in different ways. In order to help interprofessional understanding, we outline below some features of the initial education of teachers and speech and language therapists

Speech and language therapists

The curriculum for speech and language therapy focuses on human development, with particular reference to language and communication. Students undertake observation studies and learn to describe communication in considerable detail. Linguistics, the science of language, is therefore an important subject which provides skills in listening, recording and analysing examples of human communication. Linked with this, students study medical and biological sciences and psychology in order to understand human structure, development and behaviour. The main focus of interest is communication difficulty and how this can be alleviated. There is considerable emphasis on the individual. Specific 'professional studies' for speech and language therapy are concerned with students' own communication skills and how they will function in their 'clinical' role.

The influence of the health service is apparent when therapists refer to individuals as 'patients' and their work settings as 'clinics'. They engage in 'diagnosis' and 'prognosis' and frequently conclude that a person has a 'disorder'. This terminology does not sit happily in educational settings, and therapists and teachers may wish to discuss this together.

Teachers

Teachers' initial professional education may be through either a first degree or a postgraduate certificate following a degree in one or more subjects. The main focus of their training is the teaching and learning of subject(s) and other aspects of the curriculum. A considerable emphasis is placed on the organization of learning and the management of groups of pupils with a range of abilities and needs. Importance is increasingly placed on 'differentiation' of approaches to meet individual needs in the classroom. It is important to note that all teacher training courses are required to have a component on special educational needs, although the amount of this, and the experience of special educational needs in practice, will vary. Specialist training, for example, for special educational needs co-ordinators, or for teachers of pupils with particular special educational needs, is at post-qualification level.

Views of language and language difficulty

Study of language difficulty reflects a range of theoretical approaches to the subject and practitioners may favour certain 'models'. We outline below four approaches which have varying degrees of prominence. The first three have traditionally been the approaches used by therapists and the fourth is mainly identified in education. Excessive emphasis on a single approach can be limiting and can prevent understanding by professionals who attempt to work together. In particular, they can create barriers between therapists and teachers.

Medical approaches

As with other aspects of special educational needs, early approaches to speech and language difficulties were influenced by medical explanations of the problems. The traditional medical approach attempts to explain a problem by identification of its cause and symptoms. Importance is placed on identifying the problem and giving it a name, a diagnosis, which suggests measures to be taken. This will be an appropriate step where there is a clear cause and course of treatment. For example, it will be necessary to identify and reduce the potential effects of ear infections, structural problems such as cleft lip or palate, or difficulties with movement or breathing. Many speech and language problems cannot be precisely labelled and the relationship between causative factors and linguistic 'symptoms' is not direct. Further, medical diagnosis will give little indication of educational need, but may suggest some measures to reduce potential effects.

While it is necessary to consider whether there are any physiological factors contributing to particular speech or language characteristics, this view cannot provide a comprehensive picture of communication difficulties or speech and language difficulties. It has only limited use in classroom settings, where it is more important to consider the interactional aspects of language and the implications for learning and thinking. The use of terminology associated with medical approaches may be a particular disadvantage to speech and language therapists working in educational contexts.

Linguistic approaches

Approaches which consider linguistic behaviour have gained influence in the past 20 years. The emphasis is on the detailed description of communicative behaviour rather than on causes or pathology. Procedures have been developed for the detailed analysis of the content, the form or the function of language which enables practitioners to pinpoint specific aspects of a difficulty and assists decisions about where to start teaching or therapy. The study of linguistic sciences is a major component of courses in speech and language therapy, but the use of the associated complex terminology may be a deterrent to effective collaboration with educational professionals, who may see language in a very different way.

Cognitive approaches

Another approach now increasingly used, particularly by speech and language therapists and educational psychologists, is based on attempts to understand how people process language. This approach combines ideas from cognitive psychology, linguistics and neurology, focusing on perception and memory and their roles in reception, storage and reproduction of information in developing speech and language. Dockrell and McShane (1992) suggest that, although children may be grouped according to overall patterns of language performance, each has a unique pattern of language abilities. These relate to characteristics of auditory processing, working memory and cognitive processes. Children with similar linguistic profiles will have different strengths and weaknesses in language processing and will therefore respond differently to teaching or therapy. Therapy and teaching are based on use of the child's strengths in processing to tackle areas of difficulty.

Educational approaches

The National Curriculum attainment target 'Speaking and Listening' illuminates the way language is generally perceived in educational settings. 'Speaking and Listening' places the emphasis on the social process, the act of communication itself. Questions concerning the social use of language, asked by a teacher with a child-centred approach, might typically explore the interest, motivation, emotional status, situational knowledge and powers of concentration of the child whose performance in speaking and listening is a cause for concern. The influence of the National Curriculum has resulted in language development in the classroom being centred upon social interaction, verbal exchanges and the sharing of appropriate language. The language environment is regarded as being of key importance and changes to the environment are seen as the means by which language can be enhanced and developed. Most children, by the age of five years, have good syntax and vocabulary and have almost complete intelligibility. Therefore teachers see their task as developing and broadening the child's language into new areas which will sustain the demands of the curriculum.

Combining the approaches

The differences between the four perspectives are important. Broadly, they suggest the distinction between language in social context and the skills and processes underlying speech and language. They also exemplify the divide which may exist between the teacher's viewpoint and that taken by speech and language therapists.

A teacher might view a poorly- or non-communicating child as being limited by social constraints and would be unlikely to ask questions concerning underlying skills and processes. Such questions, which would be typically asked by therapists, would investigate children's understanding of word or sentence meaning, memory abilities and the adequacy and effectiveness of vocabulary, sentence construction and articulation. Clearly, both aspects are necessary since they interact. Underlying skills and processes underpin language use in social settings and, in turn, language skills and the linguistic style of individuals develop out of their experience of daily situations.

Language and the curriculum

Educational developments over recent years have edged spoken language towards the heart of the curriculum, away from the era when 'language policies' reflected almost entirely issues of literacy acquisition. This has happened particularly through the move towards learning by experience, which emphasizes language and communication as vital tools for learning (Daines, 1992). Recently, the Speaking and Listening attainment target has been revised and has moved away from its original perspective which emphasized these skills in terms of social performance, seeing children as 'participating as speakers and listeners'. Although its emphasis upon Standard English has been controversial, the changes may have served to alter the perspective in a way which is helpful by specifically identifying competencies. These are potentially much more useful when trying to identify areas of speech and language difficulty. They include:

- clear, fluent speech;
- organizing what is said;
- choosing words with precision;
- taking account of the needs of the listener;
- conversational conventions such as turn taking;
- asking questions;
- use of verb tenses;
- expanding vocabulary.

It is clearly important for teachers and therapists to understand the nature of their own perspectives as well as each other's in order to construct a flexible, negotiated approach in which a variety of issues can be addressed. While teachers need to develop the ability to ask questions concerning underlying knowledge and skills for language development, therapists need to construct situations in which these processes are embedded in meaningful situations.

Practitioners in the field of speech and language difficulties need to draw on information from a range of sources. Information from medical, linguistic and processing perspectives is important but needs to be considered from the point of view of the child, the communicative partner(s) and the context of the communication. Children's language needs to be considered in terms of other people's behaviour and what is expected. In school it will be necessary to take account, not only of the way a child communicates, but of the way other people use language. This will include the language used and demanded for the curriculum and other classroom activities. The curriculum can be full of hazards if new vocabulary and concepts are introduced without careful checking that everyone understands each new word and idea. Educational and social information will provide a context for linguistic analysis and language processing information.

Ways of working

Ways of working vary in different professions. Below we outline some of the typical ways in which speech and language therapists and teachers organize their work.

Speech and language therapists

A newly qualified speech and language therapist will often work with both adults and children but, as they gain more experience, therapists often want to specialize, either with specific communication problems or with people of a certain age. This type of specialization was, and still is, linked very closely to promotion and career development. The organization of speech and language services will vary from one geographical location to another but it is not unusual for therapists who work with children to visit several different locations each week. The therapists who work with children in special schools or units often spend the majority of their time in school but need an administrative base during school holidays or at the end of the day. The most common base in many areas is a health centre. This reflects the fact that the majority of speech and language therapists in many areas are part of the NHS. If a school-age child needs speech and language therapy but a therapist does not come into their school, the child will be seen in a school clinic or a health centre. These children often miss part of the school day to attend speech and language therapy. However, in response to changes in education as a result of the 1981 Education Act (Department of Education and Science, 1981) more speech and language therapists began to work in mainstream schools. The organization of the therapists' working week began to have much in common with that of peripatetic support teachers (Lacey & Lomas, 1993). Therapists who work in mainstream schools have more contact with teachers and some newly qualified therapists are now starting their careers in school (Roux, 1996).

Speech and language therapists providing a service to mainstream schools often have to juggle the demands of headteachers, NHS administrators and parents. In some areas a small number of therapists can be responsible for 30–40 schools. Visiting children in these different schools is effective if time can also be spent with the teachers. However, this may be viewed as time-consuming by NHS administrators who expect therapists to see a specified number of children during a given period. Although teachers are keen to ensure therapy provision for those children with statements of special educational need or those at one of the stages of the *Code of Practice* (Department for Education, 1994), they do not want children to miss crucial parts of the curriculum on a regular basis when they attend a clinic.

Despite these pressures, it is true that a school provides the therapist with opportunities to liaise with teachers as they work with the children, either in the classroom or elsewhere for part of their therapy time. Children with communication problems may be seen by the speech and language therapist individually, in a group, or a mixture of the two. The therapist may see the same child several times a week, once a week or at longer intervals.

Health centre clinics are still used by many speech and language therapists. In particular, the children seen in these settings are of pre-school age and they are seen in the company of their parents.

Teachers

Schools are organized in a variety of ways and classrooms, similarly, vary in their organization according to what is perceived as being most appropriate for the planned teaching and learning experiences to take place.

In many primary, infant and junior schools, the numbers of children allow for one, two or three parallel classes for each year group ('horizontal grouping') but, in some schools, age groups are integrated, with more than one age group in each classroom ('vertical grouping'). Sometimes this is made necessary by the numbers within particular age groups, but in some schools the decision to combine age groups is consciously made as it is seen as being beneficial for the children. The rationale for this type of organization is that it allows children to develop responsibility, provides continuity in learning and allows the teacher to really get to know the children.

Some schools have an 'open plan' organization in which classes share large work areas and also have their own smaller 'home' bays or bases. This kind of organization demands a large investment of time in joint planning for both curriculum delivery and day-to-day organization and administration. However, advantages are seen to accrue in the sharing of expertise and of daily routines and tasks.

Many teachers in primary schools remain with their children throughout the teaching day, but sometimes subject co-ordinators teach their subject, for example, music, throughout the school, where it is considered that the teacher's knowledge can be employed for the benefit of all the children. When this happens, the teacher's class will usually be taken by a part-time teacher or by the member of staff whose class the co-ordinator is teaching.

Teachers have a number of organizational issues with which to contend. These include the management of the people (children, support staff, parent-helpers), the teaching time and the physical context of the classroom which they aim to make stimulating, attractive and functional. A major daily concern of the teacher is the optimal organization of the children for the purposes of teaching and learning. Decisions, which are based upon the objectives for learning, typically focus upon the employment of individual, group and class teaching strategies. Individual work is considered to foster the ability of children to work independently and take responsibility for their learning. Group work is seen as developing and enhancing social and communication skills and can also be used for teaching purposes where children are at the same stage in their learning. Whole class teaching is used to facilitate the introduction and extension of work and for other purposes such as the presentation of work undertaken by groups or individual children. There are also times when the class comes together in an activity such as PE, dance, music, discussion and story.

Teachers employ a number of criteria to group their children. From time to time it may be convenient to group by age in a mixed-aged class. Grouping may also be by the attainment level of children, who then work together on a particular task. Groups may also be formed on the basis of friendships, the aim being to promote social interaction and, possibly, the integration of potentially isolated children. Teachers also give particular consideration to children with special educational needs, placing them within supportive groups of peers to enhance frail self-esteem. There are many factors, therefore, which will guide the teacher in the organization of pupil grouping.

Teachers also have to manage their teaching time and the children's learning time effectively and they give much thought to the organization of their classrooms to maximize children's learning both when they are teaching directly and when the children are working independently.

Some schools operate what is termed an 'integrated day'. The rationale for this organization, which allows children to choose the length of time spent on an activity and to complete tasks in a chosen order, is that it will help them towards greater responsibility for, and control over, their own learning. It is therefore seen as being particularly motivating. The integrated day has been in evidence since the early 1970s and has been subject to many variations and adaptations over the years.

Most teachers would argue that there are no right or wrong ways of organizing classes and would consider that the best method is the one which is most appropriate in respect of the children in their classes and the learning experiences and activities in which they wish their children to engage. Therefore a variety of organizational strategies can be seen in most classrooms.

Collaboration in planning and management

Teachers and therapists are familiar with planning and organizing in their work. Teachers go through a process of planning, managing, recording and reporting on curriculum activities; speech and language therapists plan, organize and evaluate activities specifically aimed at developing communication skills. Where pupils experience difficulties in speech and language, the curriculum has to be planned with particular reference to their speech and language needs. The skills and knowledge of the teacher and therapist can be combined for this purpose. In these activities they can most effectively collaborate and learn from each other by linking their expertise. One suggestion is that a teacher and a therapist can act as 'critical friends' for each other, commenting on each other's work and making suggestions for change and further development.

Teams, dyads and collaboration

A school setting is ideal for teachers and therapists to work together, but the task is not an easy one. In America, Johnson *et al* (1990) urged collaboration between general and special educators as the diversity of students in the mainstream classrooms increases. The same plea can be made to teachers and therapists. However, both professionals need to recognize the limits of their training and their own professional biases in order to collaborate effectively.

Working in a multiprofessional team is challenging; the team can be made up of two or 20 people. All the different professionals are individuals and all go through a specialized professional training process and then are passed or licensed to practise. Many newly-qualified teachers and therapists look forward to closing the classroom or therapy door. They want to get on with the job and consolidate their newly acquired skills. Some professionals will choose a job where they can function as individuals. However, when people collaborate, information can be shared and new knowledge acquired. If they work in isolation, their professional growth may be inhibited.

In the Scottish study referred to earlier, on the role of speech and language therapists in the education of pupils with special educational needs, Reid *et al* (1996) describe collaboration as an 'umbrella term' which covers 'all types of situations in which a professional works jointly with, liaises with, or otherwise includes, other people who are in a client's environment in order to achieve educational or speech and language therapy aims' (p35).

The American Speech and Hearing Association (ASHA) (1991) proposed a collaborative service model for students with 'language learning disorders' in 'public' schools. They believed that no one professional has an adequate knowledge base or expertise to execute all the functions associated with providing educational services for students (ASHA, 1991). This echoes the plea from Johnson *et al* (1990) about the need to collaborate because of the diversity in the classroom. In the UK, Norwich (1990), writing about special needs education and children with communication problems, supports the collaboration between teachers and therapists because he believes that teachers do not see themselves as specialists in language and communication issues. He feels that speech and language therapists have 'quite distinct skills and knowledge in the language field'. So, when people collaborate, they need to 'share their expertise, plan jointly, work alongside each other, exchange roles and support each other completely' (Lacey, 1996, p53).

Assessment

The therapist's contribution
The ways in which teachers and therapists work together when assessing a child will depend on whether the child is already known to speech and language therapy services and whether the teacher and therapist have worked together before. If a speech and language thera-

pist is asked to see any child whom they do not already know, they will need to confirm that parental permission has been obtained before they can begin to assess the child's communication skills. The therapist will need to meet the parents as well as those involved in the child's education and will need to know their concerns and how they hope the child's needs will be met. The therapist will also want to know about the child's current patterns of communication and the way in which their communication developed.

If the referral has been made after the child begins school, the therapist will want to talk to the teacher to try to identify why an assessment is sought at this stage. They will want to talk to anyone else, such as the special educational needs co-ordinator (SENCO) or classroom assistant (support assistant/special needs assistant), who may have been working with the child. This will enable the therapist to build up a picture of the child's strengths and needs as seen by others, before the therapist observes the child in the classroom.

In the classroom the therapist, like the teacher, is interested in the ways in which the child works, how they attend and concentrate on activities and the ways in which they attract attention and talk to their peers. The therapist will note the ways in which the child plays and interacts with the other children in the class, as well as what the child does when they do not understand or if they are not understood. With older children, the therapist will be interested in their study skills, how they organize their work, take notes in lessons and the way they approach work sheets, homework or specific subject areas. The therapist will also want to discuss with the child what they see as their priorities for learning and the most acceptable ways for them to receive help: for example, in-class support, withdrawal or a short, intensive course in the school holidays.

The therapist will want to compare findings with the teacher and discover what teaching strategies work with this child. They will probably at some stage want to see the child individually to assess their comprehension and expressive skills. This may involve the use of standardized tests which provide an age-equivalent score. Such information may be necessary to evaluate future intervention and to contribute towards a statement or record of special educational need.

The individual assessment of a child by a speech and language therapist will often involve formal and informal procedures. During the assessment process, the therapist will use their knowledge of linguistics, cognition and child development to interpret test results and help establish the child's strengths and weaknesses. Standardized tests of comprehension, where all contextual clues are removed, may complement the teacher's findings from classroom observation. The same is true when the therapist analyses samples of spoken language in order to compare a child's sound system, vocabulary and grammar in spontaneous speech with examples produced in a structured setting. For example, children with speech problems are often able to produce single words or single-syllable words accurately but their speech production will deteriorate, sometimes to the point of unintelligibility, when attempting to produce multi-syllable words or during classroom conversations or debates. This can be due to the length or complexity of the conversation and the child's utterance, or to the stage they have reached in the maturation of their sound system.

The same in-depth analysis by the therapist is required when looking at a child's grammatical structures as well as their use and understanding of vocabulary. This latter area links with the teacher's observations of the way in which a child acquires new vocabulary and how quickly specific topic-based vocabulary is learned. In secondary schools, because of the range of subjects, it is important to help the child examine the strategies they already use to help their memory of new vocabulary and to consider additional strategies which could be tried.

The ways in which a child uses language skills, that is, the pragmatics of language, are best observed and noted in a group setting, which is why the classroom is an ideal venue for observation. The therapist's and teacher's observations will be closely linked at this point.

If the child is already known to both the teacher and therapist, a different pattern of assessment may occur. In this situation, any previous information and assessment results will be studied and compared with the child's current level of functioning. Reference will be made to individual education plans and to progress over the last school year. Together the therapist and teacher will try to identify areas that need reassessing and the best ways this information can be gained. In some settings, such as an infant classroom, one practitioner may carry out activities, either individually or in a group, while the other is able to observe and record the findings. In other settings, the therapist may meet the SENCO, who will represent the views of several teachers to try to establish common and realistic goals.

The teacher's contribution

Observations carried out by teachers in classrooms are an important contribution to the overall assessment of children's speech and language. The teacher constructs an appropriate learning context by means of language and aims to enhance and develop children's communication skills through the curriculum. This is so for all children and, against the backdrop of an appropriately structured linguistic environment, assessments can be made of the difficulties which are being experienced by the child; such assessments should thus exemplify the child's linguistic abilities in functional settings. Teacher assessment contributes to the investigations being undertaken by the speech and language therapist into the particular difficulties of the child. These should then result in appropriate action plans being drawn up in consultation with the therapist. The findings of both therapist and teacher will be of further use in identifying and understanding the particular difficulties experienced by the child within the curriculum, for example in reading and maths.

The value of the teacher's contribution to assessment lies in the opportunity which they have to observe the child in a naturalistic setting. Often such observations can reveal areas of hitherto unnoticed difficulty as well as adding further data to the therapist's assessment. Teachers can produce vital contributions to assessment by observing and gathering examples of the child's receptive and expressive language and of the way the child engages in communication with peers. Observations concerning language comprehension can be made by considering the child's behaviour in response to the teacher's instructions. Does the child, for example, carry out the task, or do they appear to 'disobey'? Are there misunderstandings with peers, spontaneous unrelated remarks, the seeking of verbal or non-verbal assistance, or evidence that the child has failed to grasp the point of the activity? All these classroom-based observations can provide powerful indications that the child is not understanding.

However, it could be equally true to say that the child's difficulties as outlined above may have been exacerbated by the linguistic environment of the classroom. Therefore an important part of the assessment will be the teacher's reflections on their delivery of information and instructions as part of their overall assessment of the child's functioning within the classroom.

Teachers can also collect useful assessment data on children's spoken language. They will be aware of how well they and the child's peers are able to understand the child. Examples of words collected by the teacher or classroom assistant can represent valuable data for analysis by the speech and language therapist. An often cited difficulty which teachers experience is knowing which immature realizations are acceptable at particular ages. A knowledge of the stages of development of the sound system would be extremely useful, but this is not part of most teachers' initial training, although it might be acquired at a later date through in-service training or personal reading. However, during general classroom activities, observations can be made of the child's accuracy in producing sounds, speech fluency, retrieval of words and ability to produce correct word order.

The classroom provides an excellent setting for the observation of the child who is having difficulties with the use of language for different purposes — a pragmatic difficulty. This manifests itself in inappropriate responses to communication and so, here, the teacher, observing the child in collaboration with others, can comment upon the child's ability to take turns in conversation, give and get attention, repair conversations and, in general, speak and act appropriately in the light of the activity being undertaken, particularly in relation to the timing of help given, comments made and suggestions responded to.

Teachers are very familiar with assessment and extensive record keeping. They are also particularly good at devising recording systems which are useful, imaginative and perceptive, particularly in relation to children with special educational needs. Such recording systems build up excellent continuous pictures of development. In some areas, for example in reading, single 'scores' such as reading ages or levels are seen to add little to teachers' knowledge of the nature and quality of the child's reading. Checklists can be more helpful, but suffer in general from being the product of the author's particular view of the reading process. Therefore some teachers employ their own categorization systems for observation. For example, in relation to language skills, headings might be 'the child in conversation' or 'asking and answering questions'. These can then provide an appropriate framework for assessment.

Not only will teachers be interested in assessing receptive and expressive language skills and the communicative abilities of children, but they will also be particularly interested in the therapist's findings and how any difficulties will impinge upon the child's learning: for example, the effects of phonological difficulties upon the acquisition of reading skills or the effect of difficulties with linguistic concepts such as 'except' or 'either/or' upon the development of notions of cause and effect and the ability to predict.

With regard to the development of literacy skills, there are questions which teachers can ask which will illuminate the way in which underlying linguistic difficulties may be affecting reading and writing. For example, the teacher might consider the level of the child's comprehension of word, sentence structure and topic meaning, their mastery of word-attack skills and the level of difficulty experienced in word recognition.

In relation to writing, teachers will want to note the choice and ordering of ideas and words, the quality of sentence structure, spelling patterns and handwriting facility, legibility and size. Additionally, the ease with which children can read back their own writing and the extent to which this is seen by the child as being a useful strategy is very illuminating in the assessment of underlying speech and language difficulties and their impact upon learning.

Collaboration for assessment: links with parents

Parents are essential contributors to the assessment of their child. They will have more interactions with their child in a wider range of situations than professionals and, as a consequence, will be able to provide a broad picture of their child's functioning in terms of, for example, the way in which the child generalizes learning to different situations. From this comprehensive viewpoint parents are often able to tell professionals that their child is much more able than assessments suggest. Great emphasis is placed throughout the *Code of Practice* on partnership with parents and, indeed, in involving the child or young person.

Conversely, however, the emotional involvement which parents have with their children, resulting in different ways of interacting, may produce somewhat different and less objective judgements. These may arise, for example, from anxiety concerning the child's repeated failure or challenging behaviour. Therefore one of the functions of the professional is to try to bring an objective approach to the partnership. This can only be successfully achieved if the principles of teamwork which are adhered to within professional relationships can also be extended to relationships with parents whose views, knowledge and feelings can be taken into account by the processes of negotiation and information sharing that characterize the working practices of professionals.

Individual Education Plans (IEPs)

The IEP contains teaching targets and details of methods, materials and the adults who will be involved in the child's programme. The IEP needs to draw upon the speech and language therapist's advice but be firmly embedded within the classroom context. This is very important since the learning environment is where the child functions and, if account is not taken of classroom experience, there may be a tendency for the IEP to consist of 'bolt on' activities. Because these focus exclusively upon the child, they can overload the curriculum, inhibit the child's progress socially and result in the loss of learning opportunities.

The teacher and therapist can work productively on links between literacy and spoken language, bearing in mind that each can be used to underpin and develop the other. In work on phonology and articulation by the therapist and the teaching of phonic skills by the teacher, a common teaching system such as 'Letterland' (Wendon, 1987) can be employed, which will enhance the work of both professionals and provide a stable, memory-aiding system for the child in the early stages of learning to read. Children with both receptive and expressive language difficulties can be greatly helped through the development of their reading skills. The use of a reading scheme with a controlled vocabulary which is extended logically and progressively over time provides an effective route into reading. This, together with work on phonological aware-ness, provides a powerful means of enhancing both written and spoken language skills and as such will con-stitute a sound basis for the work which is likely to be undertaken by the therapist.

Such early work on the teaching of literacy skills will also provide a framework from which comprehension and language knowledge can be extended in terms of structure, meaning and use. For the child with speech and language difficulties, print provides a stable resource which is a teaching tool for spoken language in its own right.

When considering common objectives leading to the construction of IEPs, language issues which are embedded in the context of the classroom can be addressed by both therapists and teachers. These are that language is

a means of thinking about and responding to the world;

a powerful tool for learning;

a fundamental means by which learning contexts are created and developed by teachers;

enhanced and developed through the curriculum and other activities.

(Daines *et al*, 1996, p46)

Addressing these issues requires consideration of teaching style, the organization of contexts for learning and the manner of curriculum delivery.

In constructing an IEP for a child with speech and language difficulties, the effective combining of objectives is of key importance and may present a substantial chal-lenge to both therapist and teacher. It is necessary for the teacher to acquire an understanding of the linguistic diffi-culties of the child if their consequences are to be addressed within the child's classroom learning. This may present problems, since most teachers have little or no information on speech and language development and difficulties from their initial training and may not have had the opportunity to attend in-service courses or to work alongside a speech and language therapist. Therefore the therapist may be the only source of expertise and information for the teacher. Similarly, the teacher will be the major source of information for the therapist concerning the child's functioning in an educational setting. It is quite possible that both professionals will be uncertain about the way in which their particular knowledge of the child will 'dovetail' and schools need to understand that the achievement of productive collaboration requires the allocation of time for discussion and, thereafter, for planning and evaluation (Wright, 1996).

In addition to this collaborative picture of the nature of the child's difficulties, curriculum assessment and comment on any behavioural or emotional difficulties, the IEP should also contain an outline of strengths. Here the teacher is well placed to note naturally occurring behaviours such as those which indicate that the child is absorbing information by visual means or is using natural gesture to augment communication.

The Action Plan is the outline of the special educational provision. It needs to consider teaching style, which will encompass the creation of the learning context, the most effective means of curriculum management and teacher responses to the child. Examples of these might be ensuring that order-of-mention mirrors order-of-action, the use of gesture to aid communication and the employment of mnemonics such as colour coding.

The teacher will also need to consider pupil grouping within a variety of activities to maintain or enhance the self-esteem of the child with speech and language difficulties. The deployment of staff will also have to be organized and decisions will have to be made about ways to support the child most effectively. This often presents a dilemma for teachers who are aware of the need for support but at the same time recognize that children can be made to feel different by the constant presence of an adult. Careful planning is necessary to avoid this situation and teachers are aware of the need for clear guidelines to support staff.

Where the speech and language therapist suggests particular activities, these are most effective when incorporated into the curriculum. For example, vocabulary can be linked to topic work and expressive language targets can be supported in day-to-day situations by the adults in the classroom remodelling and expanding the child's utterances, as follows:

Child: Go zoo.
Teacher: Oh, you went to the zoo.

For older children, the activity of writing is one which lends itself well to language analysis and teaching. Here the teacher is able to discuss the use of particular linguistic conventions with the written word as a stable resource for the child.

The child with receptive language difficulties can be helped by the teacher by such means as alerting them to listen, matching the sequence of instructions to the stages of the task, checking instructions and interspersing them with visual cues, and being sure that the child knows the vocabulary that is being used. Similarly, teachers are aware of the powerful influence of their responses to children and how such responses can help or hinder the child with a speech or language difficulty. Giving the child time to respond verbally, encouraging the child's peers to do likewise and allowing the child to demonstrate understanding by visual or gestural means all give the child maximum opportunity to show that they do understand, while increasing what may be frail self-esteem.

Targets concerning the improvement of the child's intelligibility present rather more difficulty in relation to classroom activities. Since most children do not have such difficulties, it is not possible to form groups to work together and, moreover, the nature of the difficulties requires frequent guidance and support for the teacher from the speech and language therapist. IEP targets should be of a realistic number (three or four), reflect speech and language objectives embedded in the context of the classroom and curriculum, be achievable while extending skill and be understood by all concerned with the child.

At the end of an agreed period of time, teacher and therapist will need to discuss the child's progress. Targets may need breaking down or extending and there may be some that do not fit well into an approach through the curriculum. Often targets based on complex difficulties can be remodelled by the therapist to fit more easily into a classroom context.

Setting therapy objectives linked with classroom work

There are only a limited number of hours that therapists and teachers can spend with the child who has communication problems. These need to be used for maximum effect. If the speech and language therapist and teacher work together, joint goals and objectives can be identified which both professionals can work towards. This ensures continuity for the child and enables all their specialist provision to be integrated into the school day. This may be done via the work assessment, planning and intervention in relation to IEP. If the teacher is involved with the therapist in assessing a child's communication problems, and with the planning, they see the sense in the intervention and how it can be fitted into the school day.

One of the surprising issues that came out of the Wright (1994) study was the fact that therapists and teachers who worked together really appreciated what they learnt from each other. This learning may have been about different ways of working, for example classroom organization compared with one-to-one or small group work, or new knowledge, sharing of specialist knowledge and skills, and actual staff training, for example with signing being taught to teachers by the therapist. Therapists who work closely with teachers increase their knowledge of what teachers have to offer and are then able to see how the teachers' work can complement that of the therapists.

Records
Teachers keep a number of different kinds of records. These relate to day-to-day school organization, such as registers, and to all aspects of planning for teaching and learning. Such records span long-, medium- and short-term aims and objectives and will be informed by the curriculum framework and programmes of study, a large percentage of which is firmly embedded in the National Curriculum. Records which relate to pupil progress are kept to inform planning, to maintain continuity and progression in children's learning and to contribute to pupil assessment. Record keeping is, therefore, very important

and likely to be defined in a whole school policy which fulfils the legal requirement for records of attainment to be kept in each National Curriculum subject for each pupil.

Many schools collect evidence of children's learning in a portfolio for which the child and the teacher together select contributions. These can be used to highlight achievement and progress over time and to provide an indication of the breadth of the curriculum. Moreover, portfolios can also be used for reporting purposes, since teachers regularly report children's progress to parents.

Joint training: the way forward

In the introduction to this booklet, a number of publications were cited which recommended joint training for teachers and speech and language therapists. Initial professional education can only go so far and its aim is to bring professionals to a level of basic competence. There is little time in busy initial courses for many joint activities with other would-be professionals. However, professional development must continue throughout working life. The Teacher Training Agency (TTA) has endorsed this belief for teachers (TTA, 1995). The Special Educational Needs Training Consortium working party which reported to the Department for Education and Employment in 1996 suggested that, as special education can be defined as that which must be provided 'over and above' what is usually available for pupils, so certain areas of knowledge and skill will be over and above what is expected of all teachers (Special Educational Needs Training Consortium, 1996). They must therefore expect professional development opportunities which equip them to take on particular roles

31

and tasks. Teachers of children with speech and language difficulties were included as an example.

The professional body for speech and language therapists has published similar views (Royal College of Speech and Language Therapists, 1996b) and, indeed, requires its members to give evidence of their continued professional development by maintaining a 'professional log'. Continuing professional development covers a range of activities, from reading a book to undertaking a full award-bearing course. Whatever the focus, it is useful to consider how other practitioners can be involved. Where different professionals work together, participation in the same activities can enhance working relationships. The two professionals may actually attend courses together. Alternatively, where one attends a course or undertakes a development activity, other professional colleagues can be involved through discussion or engagement in specific tasks in the work setting.

There are suggestions that positive changes are beginning to happen and there is evidence of a will to increase opportunities. However, a project jointly funded by the Departments of Health and Education to examine speech and language therapy in schools concluded that 'scope for improving channels of communication at all levels was identified' (Jowett & Evans, 1996). We hope that some of the ideas presented in this booklet will promote collaboration at practitioner level.

Bibliography

AFASIC/ICAN, *Principles for Educational Provision: children and young people with speech and language impairments,* AFASIC/ICAN, London, 1996.

Alexander R, *Policy and Practice in Primary Education,* Routledge, London, 1992.

ASHA, 'A model for collaborative service delivery for students with language-learning disorders in the public schools', *Rockville: American Speech and Hearing Association* 33, 44–50, 1991.

College of Speech and Language Therapists, 'Speech and Language Therapy in Education', *Bulletin of the College of Speech and Language Therapists,* p495, 1993.

Communications Forum, *Speech and Language Therapy: Claim your child's educational rights!* (undated); available from Communications Forum, PO Box 854, 3 Dufferin Street, London EC1Y 8NB.

Daines B, 'Crossing the divide: the relationship between teaching in class and speech and language therapy programme objectives', Miller C (ed), *The Education System and Speech Therapy*, proceedings of an AFASIC Conference held at City University London, 11 July 1992.

Daines B, Fleming P & Miller C, *Spotlight on Special Educational Needs: speech and language difficulties,* National Association for Special Educational Needs, Tamworth, Staffs, 1996.

33

Department for Education, *Code of Practice on the Identification and Assessment of Special Educational Needs*, Department for Education, London, 1994.

Department of Education and Science, *Education Act*, DES, London, 1981.

Dockrell J & McShane J, *Children's Learning Difficulties: a cognitive approach*, Blackwell, Oxford, 1992.

Enderby P & Emerson J, *Does Speech and Language Therapy Work?*, Whurr, London, 1995.

HM Inspectors of Schools, *The Education of Pupils with Language and Communication Disorders,* The Scottish Office Education and Industry Department, Edinburgh, 1996.

Johnson LJ, Pugach MC & Devlin S, 'Professional Collaboration', *Teaching Exceptional Children,* Winter, 1990.

Jowett S & Evans C, *Speech and Language Therapy Services for Children,* NFER/Department of Health/Department for Education and Employment, Slough, 1996.

Lacey P, 'Supporting pupils with special educational needs', Mills J (ed), *Partnership in the Primary School: working in collaboration,* Routledge, London, 1996.

Lacey P & Lomas J, *Support Services and the Curriculum,* David Fulton, London, 1993.

Lewis A, *Primary Special Needs and the National Curriculum,* Routledge, London, 1995.

Norwich B, *Reappraising Special Needs Education,* Cassell, London, 1990.

Pollard A & Bourne J, *Teaching and Learning in the Primary School,* Open University Press with Routledge, Milton Keynes, 1994.

Reid J, Millar S, Tait L, Donaldson M, Dean E, Thomson G & Grieve R, *The Role of Speech and Language Therapists in the Education of Pupils with Special Educational Needs,* Edinburgh Centre for Research in Child Development, University of Edinburgh, 1996.

Roux J, 'Working collaboratively with teachers: supporting the newly qualified speech and language therapist in a mainstream school', *Child Language Teaching and Therapy* 12 (1), pp48–59, 1996.

Royal College of Speech and Language Therapists, *Communicating Quality 2: professional standards for speech and language therapists,* RCSLT, London, 1996a.

Royal College of Speech and Language Therapists, *Continuing Professional Development for Speech and Language Therapists: a Policy for the Future,* RCSLT, London, 1996b.

Royal College of Speech and Language Therapists, *OFSTED Inspection of Schools: Guidelines for Speech and Language Therapists,* RCSLT, London, 1996c.

Shaw L, Luscombe M & Ostime J, 'Collaborative working in the development of a school-based speech and language therapy service', paper presented to the Royal College of Speech and Language Therapists Jubilee Conference, York, October 1995.

Special Educational Needs Training Consortium, *Professional Development to Meet Special Educational Needs: Report to the Department for Education and Employment*, 1996; available from SENTC, Flash Ley Resource Centre, Hawksmoor Road, Stafford ST17 9DR.

Teacher Training Agency, *The Continuing Professional Development of Teachers,* Teacher Training Agency, London, 1995.

Wendon L, *Letterland,* Letterland Press, Cambridge, 1987.

Wright J, 'Collaboration between speech and language therapists and teachers', unpublished PhD thesis, University of London, 1994.

Wright J, 'Teachers and therapists: the evolution of a partnership', *Child Language Teaching and Therapy* 12 (1), pp3–16, 1996.

About the Royal College of Speech & Language Therapists

The Royal College of Speech & Language Therapists (RCSLT) is the professional body for speech and language therapists in the UK. It is responsible for setting, promoting and maintaining high standards in the education, clinical practice and ethical conduct of speech and language therapists.

The RCSLT:

● Monitors the education of speech and language therapists and awards a certificate to practise only to individuals who have successfully completed an accredited course. Speech and language therapy courses are at degree level and most last three or four years. There are postgraduate courses which normally last a minimum of two years.

● Maintains a register of practising members. Members are all qualified speech and language therapists who must adhere to the Royal College's code of ethics and are committed to continuing their professional development.

● Encourages research.

● Provides an information service.

● Publishes the *European Journal of Disorders of Communication*, which contains up-to-date research on speech and language difficulties.

● Publishes *Communicating Quality*, a guide to professional standards and good practice in speech and language therapy.

● Provides careers information on speech and language therapy.

The Royal College of Speech & Language Therapists can be contacted at: 7 Bath Place, Rivington Street, London EC2A 3DR. Telephone: 0171-613 3855. Fax: 0171-613 3854.

About Winslow

Winslow is a specialist publisher and distributor of practical and accessible resources for speech and language therapy, as well as other areas of education and healthcare.

Our published titles include the renowned *ColorCards* and a wide range of publications on language development, early skills, dysfluency, cleft palate, feeding, sensory & motor skills, assessment, pragmatics, phonology, social communication and other areas.

Many of these titles are valuable to both teaching and therapy professionals working with children with language difficulties. They are used in schools to facilitate a holistic approach to language intervention.

Parents will also benefit from using these titles with guidance from a speech and language professional.

Also Available from Winslow

ColorCards

ColorCards are hugely successful and popular language teaching and remediation cards. Clearly photographed and laminated for durability, there are 24 sets available. These range from basic vocabulary cards on subjects such as food, everyday objects, animals and sport to sets that specifically work on language structures, such as verbs, adjectives and prepositions. Other packs are designed for more complex areas such as listening skills, sequencing, emotions and tenses. *ColorCards* are suitable for individual and group work. A display system is also available.

Working with Children's Language

Jackie Cooke & Diana Williams
Containing a wealth of ideas and a wide range of activities, the practical approach to language teaching has helped establish this book as a leading manual in its field. Games, activities and ideas suitable for developing specific language skills make this a valuable resource for everyone working with children.

Working with Children's Phonology

Gwen Lancaster & Lesley Pope
Successfully bridging the gap between theory and practice, this book provides a wealth of creative ideas for lively and entertaining activities to use on children with phonological disorders. A stimulating and essential resource with an emphasis on clinical approaches that children will enjoy. A companion sourcebook by the same authors is also available.

Early Communication Skills

Charlotte Lynch & Julia Cooper
This is a practical resource for all professionals looking for fresh educational and therapeutic ideas in their work with pre-school children and their parents. It contains more than 100 communication-based activities, all in a photocopy-free format. A separate explanatory manual is supplied.

Early Listening Skills

Diana Williams
A highly practical, comprehensive and effective manual for professionals working with pre-school children. It is packed with more than 200 activities which are designed to be photocopied. Areas covered are auditory detection, discrimination, recognition, sequencing, memory and linking with the curriculum. Activity sheets for parents are included.

Early Sensory Skills

Jackie Cooke
A compendium of practical and enjoyable activities for vision, touch, taste and smell. Invaluable to anyone working with young children, each activity sheet contains full instructions that can be photocopied. Simple checklists are included on which to record the child's progress.

These are just a few of the many resources available from Winslow. For further information or to request a free catalogue please contact:

WINSLOW
Telford Road • Bicester
Oxon OX6 0TS • UK
Tel: 01869 244644
Fax: 01869 320040